WHAT MAKES IT GO?

Written by Rod Barkman

AIRPLANES

Enslow PUBLISHING

Published in 2027 by Enslow Publishing, LLC
2544 Clinton Street
Buffalo, NY 14224

Written by: Rod Barkman
Edited by: Beth Latham
Designed by: Amelia Harris

Cataloging-in-Publication Data

Names: Barkman, Rod.
Title: Airplanes / Rod Barkman.
Description: Buffalo, NY : Enslow Publishing, 2027. | Series: What makes it go? | Includes glossary and index.
Identifiers: ISBN 9781978548183 (pbk.) | ISBN 9781978548190 (library bound) | ISBN 9781978548206 (ebook)
Subjects: LCSH: Airplanes--Juvenile literature.
Classification: LCC TL547.B375 2027 | DDC 629.13334--dc23

Printed in China

CPSIA compliance information: Batch #QS27ENS: For further information contact Enslow Publishing LLC, New York, New York at 1-800-398-2504.

Please visit our website, www.enslowpublishing.com. For a free color catalog of all our high-quality books, call toll free 1-800-398-2504 or fax 1-877-980-4454.

Image Credits

Images courtesy of Shutterstock.com, unless otherwise stated.

Cover and Recurring – Donglpix, Synthetic Messiah. 2–3 – muratart. 4–5 – Wichudapa, Lars Christensen. 6–7 – Matchou, supakitswn. 8–9 – Skycolors, Barry-Roeland, ranchorunner, Duc Huy Nguyen, R McIntyre. 10–11 – Alexandru Nika, Nadezda Murmakova. 12–13 – John T. Daniels, Public domain, via Wikimedia Commons, Devon SA, Royal Air Force official photographer, Public domain, via Wikimedia Commons. 14–15 – Alexander Fedosov, T. Gorhum. 16–17 – Real_life_photo, supakitswn. 18–19 – ProleR, Pamela Au. 20–21 – Wirestock Creators, Gorodenkoff. 22–23 – MBekir, buradaki.

CONTENTS

WORDS THAT LOOK LIKE THIS CAN BE FOUND IN THE GLOSSARY ON PAGE 24.

WHAT IS AN AIRPLANE?

An airplane is a type of vehicle that can fly. It has wings that are fixed in place. An airplane is heavier than air, and it is usually powered by a jet engine or propeller.

Have you ever been on an airplane?

The main body of an airplane is called the fuselage. The wheels on the fuselage are called the landing gear. The flaps and tail of an airplane help control its flight.

AIRPLANES IN EVERYDAY LIFE

Airplanes are used for all sorts of things. Most of the time, they are used to move people or things from one place to another. When a plane carries objects, these objects are called cargo.

This airplane is being loaded with cargo.

Airplanes are also used to do research so that scientists can understand more about the world. An airplane might be sent to find out things about clouds, storms, or even the edge of space.

Airplanes can be used to save lives, such as airplanes that put out forest fires.

TYPES OF AIRPLANES

Airplanes come in all shapes and sizes. Have you seen any of these airplanes in the sky?

Jumbo jets are big, jet-powered airplanes that can carry hundreds of passengers.

Single-engine airplanes are much smaller. They are often used by pilots who fly on their own for fun.

Private jets cost a lot of money and usually carry less than 20 people.

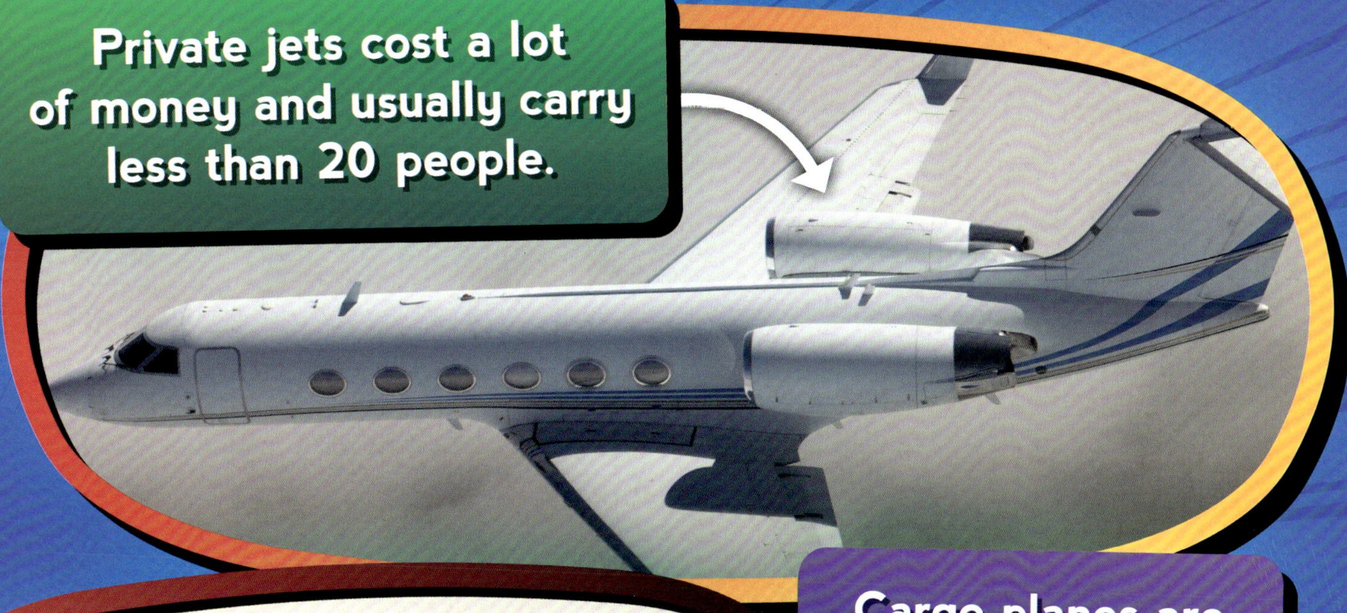

Cargo planes are made to carry objects. They have lots of space inside to hold goods.

Seaplanes can take off and land on water.

ON THE INSIDE

The pilot controls the airplane from the cockpit. Inside is a yoke, which is like a steering wheel. It is used to make the airplane go higher and lower or roll left and right.

There are lots of instruments in the cockpit. These instruments tell the pilot important things such as the airplane's speed, flying height, and direction.

INSTRUMENT PANEL

SOME ENGINES ARE CONTROLLED WITH TWO LEVERS OR KNOBS: THE THROTTLE AND THE MIXTURE.

HISTORY

The first working airplane was built and flown by two brothers, Orville and Wilbur Wright. They had been building and flying gliders for years before they built an airplane powered by an engine. Their first flight was in 1903.

Early airplanes were powered by propellers. The first jet engines were invented in the 1930s. By the 1950s, jet-powered planes were flying over the Atlantic Ocean. Over the years, jet-powered airplanes have become faster and safer.

The first jet engines were invented separately in Britain and Germany around the same time.

HOW DO AIRPLANES STAY IN THE AIR?

The main reason airplanes don't fall out of the sky is the shape of their wings. Airplane wings are curved in a special way. This means that more air hits the bottom of the wing in flight.

The shape of the wing is called an airfoil. It lets air flow smoothly over the top.

Air pressure is how much air is pressing on something. There is more air pressure underneath the wing than on top. This force from below is called lift, and it keeps the airplane in the sky.

The angle of the wing is also important, usually slanting slightly upward.

HOW DO JET ENGINES WORK?

Air is sucked into a jet engine by a big fan. The air is then squeezed by spinning metal blades. This tightly packed air goes into another part of the engine called the combustor.

The blades in a jet engine spin very quickly.

In the combustor, the air is mixed with fuel and lit with an electric spark. The mixture burns, and gases blast out of the back of the engine. The force of the blast pushes the airplane forward.

SCIENCE OF AIRPLANES

Lift is the force that pushes the airplane up. However, lift only happens when the airplane is moving forward through the air. The airplane must be shaped in a way that allows it to move through the air easily.

An airplane's pointed nose and slim shape make it more streamlined.

The force that slows something down as it moves through air is called drag. Many airplanes have flaps and slats on their wings. Pilots can move these flaps and slats to change the amount of drag.

Flaps and slats are often used during takeoff and landing.

SAFETY

Flying in an airplane is very safe, and there are lots of reasons why. Even if an engine broke while in the air, airplanes can glide a long way without power thanks to lift.

It is very rare for an engine to break. Most airplanes have more than one engine as a backup.

Air traffic controllers help keep everyone safe. It is their job to track where airplanes are so they don't get in each other's way. They talk to pilots and give them information.

Air traffic controllers make sure everyone is flying safely.

THE FUTURE

Airplanes create a lot of pollution, which is bad for the planet. Scientists are researching new types of fuel which do not create as much pollution. There may also be more electric airplanes in the future.

In the future, airplanes might not harm the planet at all.

Spaceplanes fly through both air and space. Right now, spaceplanes generally don't take off from a runway like airplanes do. But in the future, this might change!

You've learned a lot about airplanes. What kind of future airplane would you like to see?

GLOSSARY

angle	the distance between two lines that meet at a point
force	a push or pull on an object
gases	things that are like air, which fill any space available
instruments	devices used to measure things, such as speed and height
passengers	people who are carried in or on something that is moving
pilots	people who control flying vehicles, such as airplanes
pollution	harmful and dirty things being added to the environment
propeller	a rounded blade which spins to move air or water
research	studies done to find out new information
streamlined	able to move through air or water quickly

INDEX